Whore

Whore

Poems by

Sarah Maclay

[signature]

8|31|6

🏛 UNIVERSITY OF TAMPA PRESS • TAMPA, FLORIDA • 2004

Cover photograph: "Installation," 1999, by Rocky Schenck
Copyright © 2004 by Rocky Schenck
From the book *Rocky Schenck Photographs*
University of Texas Press (ISBN 0-292-70217-5)
http://www.rockyschenck.com

Manufactured in the United States of America
Printed on acid-free paper ∞
First Edition

The University of Tampa Press
401 West Kennedy Boulevard
Tampa, FL 33606

ISBN 1-879852-96-9 (cloth) ; ISBN 1-879852-97-7 (pbk.)

Browse & order online at
http://utpress.ut.edu

Library of Congress Cataloging-in-Publication Data

Maclay, Sarah.
  Whore : poems / by Sarah Maclay.-- 1st ed.
    p. cm.
  ISBN 1-879852-96-9 (acid-free paper) -- ISBN 1-879852-97-7 (pbk :
acid-free paper)
  I. Title.
  PS3563.A317974W47 2004
  811'.54--dc22
                              2003026328

Contents

For the Beloved

Better this immersion than to live untouched.

–Lynda Hull

Azure and white; I couldn't tell
my solitude from love—

–Louise Glück

feminine, winter, cold

When the blue shadows
pull themselves across the hills
and white sinks into twilight—

the blue snow of twilight—

there is an illusion of beginning:

here, where the field intersects the sky
beyond the fence;

where the crystals slowly scurry
from the firs.

It is a foreign house.
There is nothing to unpack.

It is not yet night
and the day, with its covered mouth
that refused to talk—

that day is gone:
it is a blessing.

Let it be a blessing.

Let the fir branches softly shake their snow:
soft as plumes, soft as ostrich feathers.

Bourbon

Fireflies, the dark heat,
a deep humidity begins evaporating

and night is dented with this small array of stars
from a motel—*Stardust* or *Star-Lite*,

I can't remember now.
The bones of your body—dear cage

for keeping you.
The way they make your body old

beneath your muscles. Almost ghost
limbs. Trunk of a small car, clicked open, metal

in that slow *plié*. Our fingers grip
the handles of our luggage, pull it from the dark.

Your hands. Your mother,
a whole family

crowds into the room with us.
It's summer. We unpack.

The contents of our suitcases
are mingling . . . this seems right.

A Crescendo of Rain

Tonight, I don't resent the party sounds at the end of the street
but I am wrong about the iris—
it has no stamen, which you prove
by splaying me apart
as if I'm made of legs,
made of petals—

I am made of leggy petals
and you grasp them.

&

The flannel-clouded sky a white quilt
gathered and twisted, the whole sky
a bed.   An apricot

so ripe it falls apart
in my hand, its splitting
not so much a splitting
as a falling open.

Even blue, the sky is full of rain.
The pavement sweats.

I learn to suck nourishment
from your flat, ocean breast.

Deep spring. Piano. Glass.
Lightning, a rumor of thunder
as though the curtains had moved in the wind.
(A rumor of thunder.) The sage,

the feather, the guava, the rain
and the period blood release

all at once. A mourning
dove is moaning something
I no longer know.

Wind is blowing a flag of begonias.
Wind is blowing the white gladiolas.
Ocean of salt, ocean of roses.

Street Without Street Lamps

Now the moon is back, announcing itself,
a little unwelcome.

Several days without reflection
end—even the moth's wings shine.
The windows develop streaks.

Not that the moon is a bad thing, but
I'll say it: I reject this moment.

Give me, instead, the long twilit sky
that makes the tree line ripple,

branches blackening into a kind of night,
hallucinating a boundary, a name.

Give me back our nakedness and light
and like the scent of knapweed—
wet, faintly sweet, like an afterthought—

give me the white sky, blushing.

My Lavenderdom

—as in, pre-flutter, that kingdom of semi-purpleness—should I
say *dome of*—that area of anti-limp, lawnless, drunk on your
fingering, unfingering—that omnivore, oh, eating now your—
even your branches, iceless, antifrozen, gazelle flying toward the
twin kingdoms of your cheekness (more at "flying buttress"),
nearly periwinkling now—that perpetrator of the semi-grunt,
grunt, instigator of the groanful demi-flood of—flutter, flutter,
post-flutter—gorge of neomauve, rich canal of sunsetish plush,
now unguardedly sub-fuschia; that private brandied eyelash
batting at you in its brashest postcool queenness, plump and
succulent as a plum—

Formerly Washington Boulevard

I'm waiting for the light to change. It changes. I drive west,
toward the liquor store where the mural of two women
stares across the street.

The one on the right is always happy,
languid, a little dumb.
I've always thought the one on the left

was sad, maybe even crying
as she raises an arm to cover her face,
but the one remaining eye

is simply looking at me,
simply open.

This is the way it looks to see the thing in front of you.
This is the way it looks to see what's coming.

Chiaroscuro

Your homes get better every night. At this site,
it's the landscaping that works against a modernist
approach—that long, swooping view down the steep
hill to the curving, flattened river and a eucalyptus
growing from the far peninsula. It's day.
The house itself is plain, a zen of wood and glass,
but finally it's the view to the back that paralyzes me—
where the time is always night, the weather cold, and the ice
trees—embezzled from another climate—sculpted
into light. And since it's always dark, the small tin avalanches
stay below the ground, a tiny mercy. You should hear coyotes
yipping, but you don't. A blender, maybe, whirring
from the kitchen. A daiquiri
for viewing day from your front porch.

*

Bribe me with your tongue—
it consecrates my narcissism.
Swindle me—
its deep sarcoma comforts me.
The singing folds I greet you with
are not an aberration. Everything on earth
will age: the dog anonymously barking
and the flood plain. Granite will.
The sea, the old, newly-wrinkled gray sea,
pungent with despair. And the dead Victrola.
Kill me then, you,
with your wet, swift wind,
with your ecstasy of ragged disappointment.

*

It's only in this moment that the whirlpool
is a hurricane—the rushing water I'm so used to now
becomes a rage of inner weather—leprosy and rain,
a dance of theft, a loyalty to exhibitionism.
And the still whinny
of the mare, the tractor in its slow procession
up the hill, the salt licks in their troughs—
gone. The grasshoppers, whose chirpings line the evening—
where? The dominant, incessant sound: from the roof,
a large tequila-soaked convention of small birds that twitter
through the night. A bedroom full of feathers.
Beaks. Claws. The remnants of whatever lives,
whatever we call life.

*

Should I cut off my arms, like Venus?
Would that help? Should I maintain a grave
stare, as my breasts write their desire
on the bare breeze? Vacuum up the fallen limbs?
With the fallen limbs? Would this naturalistic deformation
be a good enhancement to a stalled career?
(The lamb sucks warm milk from the green bottle
in the blizzard and the sand is sucked back into the sea.)
I can't con what I can't control, and wouldn't want to.
(The ewe bleats for the lost lamb. I succumb to my own thirst
for the wine of your predictable bouquet.)

*

I can't take my eyes off the ice trees. I prefer them,
even to the day. Their music is lit crystal, though
they do not move. A zephyr ruffles through them,
though the air is cold. Kidnap me. But you won't.
There is no resolution. (Your silent car. Your halved world.)
Yes, it is uncomfortable. I cannot leave. The leafless trees
are ripe with buds, the sensimillia of your fingertips
is mesmerizing and the frozen trees, so pure.
We are quake-insured, a sad thing, weatherproof,
but not impermeable. So I celebrate erosion.
My cat lies belly open.
There are no unread messages.
The fax spits its mechanistic howl.

Annunciation

The face at the edge of the bed, narrow, disembodied,
wakes me.

The face is plain, plate-like in dimension, almost swarthy.

Listen: there is fighting going on
in a foreign language,
a bawling child.

Harder: what is carried

like a seed, inside.

Something Thrown Away

The dogs upstairs are whirling around the living room
again. The green fruit hangs like a set of ornaments.

Heat presses me further into the sofa.
Tiny wind.

Now the air is ripped
by the breath of a passing helicopter.
Someone smashes eggshells on the counter
in another room.

Somehow, it is night again and I haven't seen it fall.
In the quiet summer moonlight, there is snow
on the banister. Ivy falls
across the wooden staircase to the deck.

This is what I plan to do:
I'll put on my black wool coat
and walk across the patio,
barefoot on cement.

It could be any season.

Rush of water as if the house
is taking a long shower.

A slight chill.
Bushes of stars. Wilting.
From a long way up:

dry avocado leaf
falling like a carefully delivered gift.

*

Eucalyptus flickers into the car.
It is hard to steer. I lose my bearings
somewhere after the first baseball field.
The cat is bored, beside me:
sophisticated, in her cage.

Through the drooping, tired trees,
sunset spreads like a bruise.
It is as though the fire leaps from the valley to the top of the
    mountain.
Like an angry curtain.
This is the view.
The pump is broken.

I don't know where the stars are.
There is an unwanted call.

Prayer to the Moon

O moon, hanging in the blank sky
Like a single ornament,

As though you had no weight

Curved like a eucalyptus leaf,
Lucid as a coin

O moon, oh reflection that does not blind,
Giving off your sliver of light

As the thin screen of day narrows
To a blue line—

A curtain sails in the last wind

And darkness falls across the ground,
Exhausted—a shadow

Quietly drained of human form

Seeping into the dirt,
Into the small fingers of grass

And rising then, into the trees,
The few small sparrows taking flight

As night uncoils its deep agave glove—

O moon, honey in the sky,
Watch over us

Even as we pause, suddenly fragile,
Suddenly kind.

Night Song

Spring; the air is October.
The night-swathed maples linger in mid-breeze

and everyone seems to be sleeping
or away.

And my belly, the whole middle of my body
swells, as when I carried you—

or later, like your body
as it passed into night.

I was your mother,
and night passed through me, into night.

No one can touch me.
No one can touch me.

LP

Sirens curling flatly in the phonograph night—
anything to fill the distance—
as the album stretches out like a thin dark lake
and the needle tears the air
with its long black moan
as it ripples along the vinyl
curve of silence.

This is the lake I skate into,
knowing it is endless.

In another room, in another house,
someone plays a piano
memory of 1975
over and over. It is the vase
we pour ourselves into. It is no substitute
for flesh. It will not stop the night.

And so the slow glissade begins,
the blades ticking backward
on the ice

while the needle knows the lake beyond the song.
The record plays long
and the needle is attentive.

Lazarus, Himself

The boxing ring of his heart is vacant,
visible through his now invisible skin.
There is more than one kind of death
and this is the headless kind,
the kind that disintegrates balls,
chips away at pieces of leg.
This is the kind that leaves a torso
perched near a lake, suspended
slightly and cocked aslant
to indicate torque. It's not
that the bones are shards,
but little cyclones,
and it's as though
the man was about to get out of the bath
if only he had arms
below the elbow; if
below the knees, he were not in need
of prosthetic devices. His clavicle
presses into the soot of a cloud
that all but lids the sky, pressing
toward the base of the tub
like a coffin—though, to the left,
there's still that view of the cliff:
rock as rocky as his body.
And now the trick is that this—
imagine, even this—
is about to be resurrected.

Daphne at the Moment
of Transformation

But now, my toenails grow into shale.
Veins root. A bleeding rock.
The gutted, pocked bark
of my shin. And birds,
sparrows, land along my
shoulders, trailing
their little worms. Leaves
spurt out of my
rugged, bone twig-knuckles.

He is running.

And the wind blows through my mouth
like hair.

Proximity

Sunday of power lines and the rooftops of industrial buildings—
smeared sand. Sky of Marseilles, Rothko-blurred,
smudges of gray. Weather, oily and warm

beneath the bluster. Empty parking lot,
its staged trees, brave, year after year, becoming
shapes open to everything, near one another,

alone. And the white dog, waiting for me all morning
by the door, so I could touch her,
who now follows me all the way to the gate

and whimpers as I leave. Sunday of wrappers
stuffed in the shrubbery, condoms left on the steep
street with the view of the lights thrown on the lawn.

And the scene on Hauser: couple of cops
dressing down a pedestrian; boy on a skateboard,
oblivious, happy; a woman

and her daughter selling roses
wrapped in transparent foil, carried like torches,
like crowns.

Car stripped down to a back seat and fender.
Sunday. Sycamores. And the coin-shimmy
silver eucalyptus. Sunday of stirring leaves. And the dead

squirrel I found near my apartment, but didn't bury in time
to save from the flies, its head removed and its tail
now beginning in a long squeeze of yellow and burnt

sienna. Reggae and violins, Sunday
a slow progression of minor chords, every plant
a burgeoning cargo of spring in the lumbering

humidity, in spite of wind.
This is the record of what is near,
against the din of the missing.

And the moth, pounding itself again, again,
against the window pane, filled with its chill light.
And the cat, removing the moth's wing. And the blur

between what is outside, what is in, like the buzz
of a trapped hummingbird and the blossoms, impossible blossoms.

90 Degrees

Magnolias bloom like a lie. Everywhere,
even, it seems, where there should only be leaves.
Splayed in the heat, beyond wilting,
no muscle to glue up the opening, spent.
More satisfied than flaccid. Ready
for a feast of flies. Oh the ivy,
the ivy, insistent,
curls through the fence from another yard.
Admit it. There's no stopping it—
whatever yard you're in,
the petals cover the darkness
like lost stars.

Adagio & Mirage

In the back, off Sierra Bonita—"Beautiful Saw"—
the lawn is leafblown to green, and by the computer
the cowboy cup is beading, hot, imprint of faded lipstick
kissing its edge. Before pulling the phone cord

from the jack, you glance again at the inbox,
beg for that heroin flip of the bold-print scroll
while scanning the scarred opera poster hung on a wall—
profile of an Egyptian woman, green face,

plenty of kohl, rainbowed headdress, hint of a claw
at the clavicle, hint of a goblet. Somebody mythic.
Must be Aida. Rolling the warm mug across your cheek,
gazing directly into the darkening suns of Aida's breasts,

you're not mythic, only an export item
from the Rockies. Somebody's bad habit
for too many years. For weeks you've been reading
a book by Lynda Hull, jumping around,

returning to Hull in a *pensione*
by the baths, in winter, delirious, finding
a vein. You've spent too long an evening
marking tests connecting word with meaning:

mirage: a slowly moving passage of music or dance,
adagio: optical illusion, appearance of something
not really there—a dream like the stick couple
gliding in shadow, hand in hand up the edge

of the picture. The bathroom is stained with
a glaze of water-ruined blue, beyond
repair. Lynda sways,
a needle in one hand, her face studying

the strange, reflected light in a mirror, buzzed
to a swooning peace. You wash your hands
in the sink, the water is tepid, you peek
through the curtains, beyond the fence where

the whole town is glamour-fatigued. Sierra Bonita
rustles with morning, a couple of neighbors
starting their cars. The gardeners climb
as usual, to the deck, then crowd the patio

of your basement apartment, blowing dirt under the door.
They rake the leaves and clippings into piles to feed
to the trash. You know that Hull will crash, flip off
the interstate into the tree, into the orange mouth

of flame; that soon she won't be able to tell
black ice from road. The logoff warning
flickers so you click on that aging message that says
you're luminous and gorgeous, says you're nothing

but loved, and time and distance collapse into adagio
and mirage as you glide toward the weathered mirror
leaning on the counter where your worn and thinned-
out face shines back, illuminated, oddly, from within.

(after Lynda Hull's "Adagio," in homage)

Whore

It comes from *hore* in Old English,
hora in Old Norwegian,
but the Latin references charity—
at the root it's *carus*—dear,
as in *Hello, whore. Hello, dear.*
As in loved one, sweetheart, precious,
as in rare—therefore expensive, dear,
cher, cheri, a luxury
when given freely,
pitting charity against law.

Driving Home Alone
After the Strand Reading

The boulevard is a blank field
and there is a fence post—old,

stuck there, holding up the fence:
that is its job. The fence

lets things through—air through,
flies, snowflakes, men climb through,

but the fence doesn't move.
Facts, facts. This is the city I live in,

this is the country, this is the boulevard's
weather. What I report to myself

is a kind of rain, a kind of ruin.
No one enters the picture; then

a black sedan, decked with ribbons,
turns down the road to the veterans' cemetery.

Black metal, black glass, white ribbons, black air,
the markers stand like rows of teeth.

Boulevard, wind, fencepost,
blaring streetlight, black flattened grass.

Plane Poem

The strobe (night   day   night)

snow   wing   barn.

The barn that's always with you.

Its two dark eyes.

The yellow lantern

doubled in the window glass.

The plane plays a long, sustained chord

like a stuck harmonica.

Organ pipes. A pack of cigarettes. A minor fourth.

Canned wind funnels down.

And there's that other sound—

of a tunnel, through a hollow bone.

Chill

It's time to cut the roses back,
time to hope for rain—

that is, to hope for a shroud

(the agate sky shifting
  in the dull winter light)

time to pare things down to nothing,
time to hope for nothing

as for any other thing:

(the cloud's surface could be glass,
  clouded glass)

I mean, as I would hope for a lover,
time to hope for nothing, in that same way—

time for the wet dirt only

(against my will, the clouds are
  suddenly shot with light)

Imagine a great stone angel with blank eyes.

As if night is a black pearl

And I can out-awake it

All the while I betray you
even by what I choose to read.

What are years?
Pieces of paper with stars on them.

I was going to say
as if the *moon* is a black pearl

but it has already
spread over everything.

Out-of-Love City

Well, here's the bowl of tightly-closed pistachio nuts, the empty bottle
of balsamic vinegar, a dozen wine glasses or so, cheese slicer on a
slab of marble, sunglasses—unfolded, upside down; matches—used,
not tossed yet; coffee filter full of grounds and orange peel, water
running over a hard-boiled egg, favorite coffee cup, beaten-up high
heels in walking position, change, bow tie on the table, index cards
and rubber bands, goggles, picture frames, wire connecting plug to
modem, candle remnant, sympathy cards—unsent, pile of cocktail
napkins, half a glass of something, 3:23, someone coughing, back of
the mail truck rolling down, sweatpants, maps—frayed at the folds;
chairs that stayed too long at the party, irises choking on their swill,
pistachio shell the cat has chased across the glossy floor.

Last Poem

Sharp light on cinder block. *Sea Mist*
is what they would call this color
in a fancier kind of town.

Simple bed. Scarred and dented
with names like *Woody*. Tobacco
seeps invisibly through the open window
and settles into the sheet I draw
across my ankles as night
finally cools.

In this room of sharp shadows,
they have not been able to rip the magpies'
talons from your epaulets.

Just as the birds flew between us
in their queer, frightening squalls,
and after all our speaking,
neither of us spoke . . .

Here you are. Silent as a photograph.
Nothing but crows between us.

Notice that I still believe, if you were really here,
that you would love not just my body,
but my shadow.

As I turn from the harsh light, my silhouette
enlarging on the wall—

but you are feathers.

Absinthe

The awning in tatters. Glowering sky.
Orchid. Simple breeze.

A woman in sunglasses, smoking,
waiting for the bus in shoes from the 50s.

Balconies meant to look like Spain.

(. . . under the glass of the greenhouse,
 hidden behind the terrarium . . .)

The clock has turned its face.
Time is silver.

Fallen on the green lawn, hundreds of oranges
in a fit of croquet,

smashed, pecked upon
by pigeons.

The door rests on its side, slowly
darkening to moss.

Curtains, cheaper than therapy.
The gray lie of asphalt.

Once is enough.
And no, no, not the golden beginning.

A dry cold . . .

A dry cold. City lies at the base of the hill like a
lake. I try to memorize the lights. Sea that is not a sea, fog, muffle
of rushing cars. At any moment.

The Rite-Aid at Fairfax and Sunset is filled with cut-rate ghouls, right
on schedule, same as any other year. Outside, the woman asking for
bus change is missing most of her teeth. Why do I think I need to
hear her obvious request?

Flags drape over tailgates like they're recipes for god. Sky as vacant as
memory. So simply. We could, they could drain the basin. One could.
I buy gum and a light bulb.

For instance, now.

What We Leave Behind

Valets untuck their shirts
before the wedding
guests arrive,

as I, who am not invited, cross
the grounds in tennis shoes and shorts

to hike the terraced Buddhist gardens
higher up the hill,

to the hidden spots
where gangs have scrawled graffiti,
where the chapel-hut is now fenced in;

to the top of the canyon,
where there's a view of the city
serpented by smog

and its dried-out hills
and the shifting downtown skyline

where birds plummet from the tops of buildings
like tiny men

in formal suits
and rust appears in the mirrored
pool by the curb

and I, who am not invited,
pass the altar of this private ceremony—

not the one about to occur,
but the one that must have happened:

she has left the clippings of her hair
on a concrete bench
in front of the mansion,

left the ends of her hair in scraps
like stray, abandoned twigs.
She must have knelt.

Fields of Salt

They ask a falling into them, their cold
weight of stars, white sifting

through the stray trees

jutting up like crippled rakes. Otherwise,
this is a figureless landscape

as it must be

and the skin, scraped clean
by scabrous, grating jewels—

each dripping across the body
in its tiny river.

And the bramble and the stooped and
segregated weeds poking into the night

can join the night.

Everything you needed: no longer there,
or necessary.

And, for once, the moon is buried
under the hill.

The Marina, Early Evening

The sea is only a blue sand,
reaching over its brother.
The sand is only a hard, brown sea.

Gulls open their beaks and nothing comes out.
One. Another. Three. The sea

is only a low cloud
wandering under its sister.
The cloud is only a high, gray sea.

The gulls seem to be praying.
They stand as still as a chess set.

Waves crawl onto the body, slither back.

Oh, the woman with red hair,
legs as tall as stilts,
sings into the ocean.

Her song is only the mirror
of the broken wave.

Why Do We Wear Clothes?

This is the child's question the story
begins to answer.

No, it isn't because of the weather.
Not today.

Because I'm beat and the body sags.
To hide that.

Because we're as human as tin
and iron and silver.

You want to go back to that other story,
the one with the fruit and the snake.

We wear them to cover the slagheap.
Because of the rugged night.

Because we dragged it up from the beach
and the seaweed followed.

Because of the something that departed,
the something that cradled us.

To hide our nakedness, because
it doesn't have a name.

We wear them because *we* departed, because
we thought we had to depart.

We are more expensive
than we know.

And we wear the tale more tightly
than our clothes.

Well, quit

telling yourself that story
so that it can change.

(I hope this comes across as dark and painful.)

The Waters

A brown morning, dawn a singed sky, the day already sepia
below deserted bridges, oars breaking water
near the 16th *arrondisement*,
                         a black boat, single rower,
the Louvre goes on for centuries, water climbs the walls:

it's a woman standing at the oars,
who doesn't like what she sees ahead,
but steers toward it, pointing the vessel west—
                         west in the desolate quiet

like a vision or a ghost—
through catkins ready to shed their seed,
                         the silhouettes of skyscrapers,
monolith blocks translucing just beyond cloud,
world gone suddenly thin
                         as the page of an advertisement—

a cipher for the light show, a screen
floating along from *piazza* to *plaza* to place,
                         from *cielo* to *ciel* to sky.

               This is how we wake, at the helm of a small boat—
alone in the city,
alone in time and the artifacts of time and the names
         we inherit and learn,
                    in our white shift,
in an element liquid, viscous, reflective,
                         as colors from solid objects streak
across what cannot be pinned down—

before the day begins and water
                washes its lodge of carrion
against the banks
                and the world is almost black and white,

before we're backlit,
                once again, by fire.

What "I" Dream To Save "Myself"

In the bare alcove of a shared
      dorm, taking a bottom bunk,
            I can make myself content, I think,

until I'm coaxed
      into the suite of rooms next door. It is a sign,
n'est-ce pas?, to see my blond ex-friend,
      clothed in the plummish
            velvet and white-feathered tight-fitting jacket of some lost
                  decade—lost before either of us were born—

stepping from the Greyhound
      with an air of easy inheritance and a kind of fluffy, smug
            (and matching) arrogance, worn lightly.

She has come as if to a costume ball.

What interior goes with that clothing?
      I want to say indigo—just for the sound—
            but that would be a lie.
                  And of course she disappears just as

the rooms next door open onto
      a "sun-drenched kitchen," even a stable.
            I consider the stable, with its old, cut stones:
                  a daybed in the stable—
                              a simple, airy room apart.
      Yes,
            maybe near a gazebo
                  or a sunroom with its twining leaves.

And then I come to the masculine
        mahogany chamber—seems to be a drawing room—
            I try the couch and aha! it's a comfortable
                hide-a-bed which I might not consider
except for the truly unexpected view—

permanent sunrise, or is it sunset? Violet over the water,
        a palm, a mountain—
            a mountain snowy as Fuji—
                behind the lake, or bay.

It is as though a kind of hope has been scorched there.
        All contradictions can live in one place,

                and even, to the left, tall, tall as a palm tree, taller—
a clock-tower, moving its Swiss hands
        over the nearby city.

It is an illusion, but I have to admit
        it is beautiful

                and you are not even here.

Island of Bones

Well, ok, the past stripped down, hardened
into something white. Heaps of it.

And gulls, arguing mildly over the bits of flesh,
swooping into a shifting embroidery—

this way, no, this way—
as fabric changes its sheen
when pulled. If there are spiders—

white ones, tiny,
making a slow music
over the freeway of ribs,

the strange erector sets curving together
like sad shells, as hollow (without love,

all triumph is hollow)—

think of the inside of a flute:
silver, cold, the fluted breath
that blows into it, mouth a frozen kiss

but the air—specific, warm.
And it's over this island of bones that the vines
begin—begin

as we grab the past and blow
air into its hollow,
the birds be damned.

Mother-of-Pearl

So let's call them something other than clouds—
mirror, shell, flame. The sky's idea of hair.

And you know the way the voice sounds
when it's cried all day:

like it could comb stones.
Imagine, then, I'm driving to this sound

which is its own kind of rough velvet
under an amber sky, and the D.J.

has a jones for just this sort of thing tonight
as I circle the block, looking for parking

and must circle several times
because of the gray, lithe limbs,

as though a body had many arms—
and each was nearly satin, raised,

tree after tree, with its endless
offering of leaves.

This is the way I walked into our rendezvous,
carrying a miracle

in the inner lining of my pocket. So don't ask
why those kisses under the streetlamp,

borrowed moon, under the arms unable
to retreat from their suspension, permanent

in gift, don't ask why everything that followed
made me your mirror, shell, flame. I will tell you:

The sugar fell all the way to my ankles
and I had to eat.

Yard Work

I'll clear the old, putrid fruit,
the carcasses of bees where oranges have fallen
and the drying turds the dogs have dropped.
I'll sweep away the fallen avocado leaves
grown snowy with their infestations,
snip the stems of toppled flowers, toss them.
I'll yank the hose across the grass,
turn the rusty faucet,
let the lawn moisten
to a loose, runny black.
I'll water the rosemary
till I can smell it on my fingers.
Time to grab the trowel.
Time to dig,
to take off the gloves,
let the handle callous the palm,
fill the fingernails
with dirt.
Time to brush the trickle from the forehead.
Time to plant the bulb,
to fill the hole with loam and water,
covering the roots.
Time to join the soil to soil
until the night is jasmine
and a thickness like a scent of lilies
rises off the bed;
until the stalks of the naked ladies fall to the ground,
twisting on their roots;
until our broken fists lie blooming.

The Snows

Mais où sont les neiges d'antan?
                    — François Villon

As now, all around us,
                    like the feathers of lost swans,
the past sifts over the present,
                    we look out the window,
catch each other's eyes
                    —we look the same—
every mistake is forgiven,
                    the past and the present join like hands,
all other paths are forgotten—

they're here. They've always been here. They're still here.

Nothing is lost.
                    Time is only a chamber for ripening,
                                        alone, alone.

Notes

The epigraph quotation by Lynda Hull is from the poem "Frugal Repasts" in *Star Ledger* (Iowa City: University of Iowa Press, 1991); the lines from Louise Glück appear in her poem "Aubade" in *The Seven Ages* (New York: Ecco Press, 2002).

"*feminine, winter, cold*": attributes of yin, according to a small deck of Taoist cards found in a bowl on the kitchen counter at the home of a friend.

"Chiaroscuro": from the Italian *chiaro* (clear, light) + *oscuro* (obscure, dark)—generally used to describe the play of light and dark in pictorial representation, without regard to color.

"Prayer to the Moon": after 9/11/01.

"Night Song": for Dorothy Kemble, b. 1925, and in memory of Kevin Kemble, 1951-2000.

"Lazarus, Himself": after Salvador Dali's *Rhinocerotic Disintegration of Illissus of Phidias.*

"As if night is a black pearl": apologies to Marianne Moore.

"Island of Bones": after learning, of Key West, that "the island's name derives from the Spanish explorers who dubbed the spot 'Cayo Hueso,' or Island of Bones, for the scattered remains of the Calusa Indians and shipwrecked sailors they found there." (Mary Jo Vickers, U.S. Airways *Attache*, January, 2002, p. 47.)

"The Snows": the epigraph, in translation: "But where are the snows of yesteryear?"

Acknowledgements

Grateful acknowledgment is made to the editors and publishers of the following publications, in which versions of these poems first appeared:

Field: "The Marina, Early Evening"

ForPoetry.Com: "Daphne at the Moment of Transformation" and "Driving Home Alone after the Strand Reading"

Poetry International: "Yard Work"

Poetix the Magazine: "Night Song," "Mother-of-Pearl," and "What 'I' Dream to Save 'Myself'"

Pool: "As if night is a black pearl . . ."

Runes: "Island of Bones"

Solo: "The Waters" and "Whore"

Tampa Review: "Chill," "*feminine, winter, cold,*" "LP," and "90 Degrees"

Deepest thanks to David St. John, Cecilia Woloch, Mary Ruefle, Roger Weingarten, Bill Olsen, Ralph Angel, Betsy Sholl, Rick Jackson, Jack Myers, Nancy Eimers, Nance Van Winckel, David Wojahn, Jody Gladding, Ken Fox, Jan Wesley, Holaday Mason, Jim Natal, Jeanette Clough, Marjorie Becker, Amy Schroeder, Beverly Lafontaine, Mark Kemble, M. L. Colby, Bruce Boston, Brendan Constantine, Paul Lieber, Sandra Alcosser, Fred Dewey, Mark Fox, Brenda Yates, David Oliviera, Dina Hardy, Louise Crowley, and members of the Hagshop and the Saturday Workshop at the Church at Ocean Park for your support, guidance and encouragement, which allowed this book to come into being.

Special additional thanks to Ralph for guiding me through the process of assembling the manuscript, and for believing that this was, in fact, a book.

Finally, I'm grateful to the team at the University of Tampa Press for their passion and graciousness, and for championing this project: thanks to Richard Mathews for his patience, wisdom, sensitivity, and impeccable design sense; to Don Morrill and Martha Serpas for their ongoing editorial support and feedback; and to Sean Donnelly for his unflagging assistance.

About the Author

Sarah Maclay's poems have been published in *Ploughshares, Field, Hotel Amerika, Solo, Pool, ZZYZYVA, Lyric, Cider Press Review,* and many other magazines, including *Poetry International,* where she is currently the book review editor. Her critical work will soon appear in *The Writer's Chronicle.* She was a 2004 finalist for the Blue Lynx Prize for Poetry, the 2003 winner of the dA Gallery Award for Poetry, and a semi-finalist for both the 2003 Kenyon Review Poetry Prize (Zoo Press) and the 2002 Tupelo Press First Book Prize. The author of three chapbooks, *Ice from the Belly* (Farstarfire Press), *Shadow of Light* (Inevitable Press) and *Weeding the Duchess* (Black Stone Press), she also co-edited the anthology *Echo 6 8 1* for Beyond Baroque, a literary center and performance space in Venice, California, where she has been a poet-in-residence. She is a fourth-generation Montana native who grew up on a ranch in the Bitterroot Valley, later earning degrees from Oberlin College and Vermont College. She currently teaches writing in Los Angeles.

About the Artist

Rocky Schenck was born in Austin, Texas, and when he was five, the family moved to a ranch outside of Dripping Springs, Texas, where he grew up and finished high school. Starting at age twelve, he began studying oil painting, inspired by the romantic landscape paintings and portraiture work of his great-great grandfather Hermann Lungkwitz (1813-1891) and great-great uncle Richard Petri (1824-1857), both German immigrants and artists who had moved to the Texas Hill Country in 1851. He was selling his paintings professionally by age 13. At about this same time, Rocky discovered a lifelong interest in motion pictures and photography and began writing, directing and photographing low-budget experimental films. A self-taught photographer, he honed his skills while taking production stills on the sets of his movies. In 1987, a gallery owner in New York discovered his work and gave him his first one-man exhibition, followed by a second in 1990. Both shows were well-received and reviewed by influential publications, including *Art in America, Artforum,* and *Aperture.* Since then, he has continued to show in galleries around the world. He works in Hollywood as a professional photographer and his photographs are included in several prestigious collections.

About the Book

This book is set in Adobe Garamond Pro types based on the sixteenth century roman types of Claude Garamond and the italic types of Robert Granjon. They were adapted for digital composition by Robert Slimbach in consultatation with colleagues including type historian and designer Steven Harvard, letterform expert John Lane, and Adobe's Fred Brady. Slimbach and Brady have written that Garamond's "roman types are arguably the best conceived typefaces ever designed, displaying a superb balance of elegance and practicality." The Granjon italics of the same period are beautiful and graceful companions. The book was designed and typeset by Richard Mathews at the University of Tampa Press.

POETRY FROM THE UNIVERSITY OF TAMPA PRESS

Jenny Browne, *At Once*

Richard Chess, *Chair in the Desert*

Richard Chess, *Tekiah*

Kathleen Jesme, *Fire Eater*

Julia B. Levine, *Ask**

Sarah Maclay, *Whore**

John Willis Menard, *Lays in Summer Lands*

Jordan Smith, *For Appearances**

Lisa M. Steinman, *Carslaw's Sequences*

Richard Terrill, *Coming Late to Rachmaninoff*

** Denotes winner of the Tampa Review Prize for Poetry*